Dinosaur Days

written by Pam Holden

pteranodon

This dinosaur had a beak.

It was like a bird.

This dinosaur had big legs.

sauropod

It was like an ostrich.

It was like a giraffe.

This dinosaur had spikes.

stegosaurus

It was like a lizard.

This dinosaur had big horns.

triceratops

10

It was like a rhino.

parasaurolophus

This dinosaur had big claws.

It was like
a kangaroo.

This dinosaur had a long tail.

dimetrodon

It was like a crocodile.

15

dilophosaurus

This dinosaur had big teeth. Roar!